CONTINUOUS SHOWINGS

Michael Anania

MADHAT PRESS
ASHEVILLE, NORTH CAROLINA

MadHat Press
MadHat Incorporated
PO Box 8364, Asheville, NC 28814

The Library of Congress has assigned
this edition a Control Number of
2017900330

ISBN 978-1-941196-44-1 (paperback)

Cover art by Marc Vincenz
Cover design by Marc Vincenz
Book design by MadHat Press

www.MadHat-Press.com

First Printing

for Kenneth, Barbara and Ralph, unstilled voices

OTHER BOOKS BY MICHAEL ANANIA

New Poetry Anthology
The Color of Dust
Set/Sorts
Riversongs
The Red Menace (fiction)
Constructions/Variations
Two Poems
The Sky at Ashland
Gardening the Skies
In Plain Sight: Obsessions, Morals and Domestic Laughter (essays)
Selected Poems
In Natural Light
Once Again, Flowered
Sounds/Snow
Per Enzo Agostino
Turnings
Heat Lines

PREFACE

"The peculiar puzzle of desire": for love and touch, for sheer being, for music and views of the sea or of cities and farms or of the living dioramas of the past in the present—this desire is the engine of Michael Anania's "continuous showings" not only of old-time cinema but of full-time life. He's synaesthetic: he can hear a waltz—whether its three beats are straight ahead or syncopated by beboppers—as the sight of winter conifers with finches in them. He makes melody and sentence and sight his three primary colors, and he names them in his poems while simultaneously using them to mark the sharp edge—the precise and delicate edge—of his seeing and sentencing. His work evokes the jazz and classical masters (and all else) with the melody of his sentences dropping down the page through the clean-edged lines of the poem.

With grace he evokes the everyday lived reality of early and mid-twentieth-century years—his Omaha family, rough times, and gangsters, classic American films. He makes of the "tangle of causes at once / intended and accidental" something so deftly written that things seem "more likely // or more fully lit now / their edges sharpened / in the trembling air"—that is, in the air of the poem itself. From abandoned farm machinery, with its aura of long-ago use, in a vacant lot, to the evanescent edge of a flower petal, to a mid-century kid with an ice-cream cone in the midst of gangster feuds, he invites us to acknowledge, to sense, the "cascade of causalities" that carry us onward—not for our reasons but for unknowable reasons of their own.

Friends and memory, birds and cars, coincidences of delightful absurdity ("April in Paris, 1922," with Einstein, Satie, Duchamp, Marie Curie, Henri Bergson…), oranges, oaks, neon and neurons: How does it happen that any "one thing, out of

Michael Anania

so many, takes on such importance, as though life without it would seem less than life, or perhaps, in the moment, at least, less complete"? In these poems, it does take on such importance.

—Reginald Gibbons

TABLE OF CONTENTS

III.

IV.

Consider dreams, poetry, the syntax of language.
Mind everywhere is only an illustration to the running text.
—GEORGE SANTAYANA

What had been distance was memory.
—BARBARA GUEST

I

Casa de la Torre, Puerto Vallarta, Mexico

for Mark and Eszter

i.

three quartzite islands mark the Pacific
    for us, *Islas Tres Marietas*, coffee
        cups and orange peels close at hand;

here, three sculpted, winged
    Indios musicians play; one fountain
        splashes, laughter, and then another;

the propane vendor sings up
    from the street, *"gas gas,"* sea salt,
        ripe fruit and cinnamon coffee in the air,

dos viejas out on the sidewalk
    in lawn chairs; diesels ping sharp finger
        music over the cobblestone hum of truck tires

ii.

calla lilies and bougainvillea, yellow
    trumpet flowers trellised against
        a blue wall, palm fronds sighted above

moss-greened roof tiles and white-
    washed stucco; a laurel tree,
        arrayan, archaic and quick with birds—

ynca, the yellow-splashed,
    green jay clamoring among finches,
        an indigo mockingbird, anhingas circling

the tower, Moorish against stray
    clouds, *Nueva Galicia* recalled in stone,
        Jalisco noisy at its morning business

iii.

fresh laundry sways the middle
    distance; the Bay of Banderas furls and unfurls
        its light morning squalls like banners still;

Los Jorobados, whale's breath
    blown out above incoming wavelets, ,
        humpbacks arching in unison; tail flukes

lift and pause; each set of white
    markings, symmetrical and unique,
        offers its brief signature above

the indistinguishable whitecaps;
    sounding, they slip away, leaving, as they
        thrust downward, a flat, whale-marked span of sea

Michael Anania

iv.

beneath the quick city Spanish that ripples
   over the uneven streets, tones of Huichol
      and Cora like whale songs under wavetips;

along the Malecon, *mariachis*,
   the word itself held like bright yarn
      pressed into beeswax, colors fingered

into place, their names sounded out
   under the dense canopy of upland trees;
      in shop windows, four hundred years

after Guzman and Mendoza, peyote-
   radiant jaguars and spirit masks thread
      mountain to sea, coral to orchid and anemone

v.

Chela hums above tap water,
    Eszter whistles *"Cielito Lindo"*
        into the terraced garden; butterflies—

cloudless sulfurs and spring azures—
    lift and fall as though tracing the song
        against stonework; beauty, it says, descends

from the Sierras, dark eyes without tears;
    the Huichol, the healers, have walked
        white-tailed deer back into the forest

to cure us; mountain streams tinctured
    with damp bark and leafmold tumble seaward
        carrying the land's scent to whales and dolphins

Michael Anania

The Mirror of Simple Spirits

In the Barberini, *Narcissus* gleams
with varnish, its reflected light washing
away both faces, the one leaning in,
the other staring back, an accident
of paint and incandescence in which
the sheen meant to create physical depth
and figurative space shimmers them away,
both selves slipped into a disordered brightness.
This is how we make our way from simple
glare to radiance, what it is we glimpse quick
in polished surfaces, not ourselves so much
as the fray of self, the ease with which its
familiar certainties tremble and dissolve
like sounds hollowed by their own echoings.

Daffodils

for Deborah Pease

They come to you, as spirits might,
compounded of light and eagerness.

The day seems filled with consequence,
its radiant causalities drawn,

like filaments, across the room,
window shade to table's edge,

lampstand to cuticle, water
glass to mirror, doorknob to chair.

What can you say, or do even,
but wait for the wonder to subside,

breathe evenly until your eyes
adjust, relaxing, just now, with regret.

Michael Anania

Transactions of the Ingenious World

"of stuffe and forme perplext"
for Joseph Harmon

I.

This is the spring in which our Sun *must dy.*
light, itself, elongated, its colors
like feathers, wings spread and lifting; air moves,

water moves, the Venus-remembering waves,
her touch flared like heat along hammered steel,
red, yellow and blue surging inward, fired and struck;

begun in consequence, the blade from ore
and calder, the ore from pick, the pick from ore,
each beginning laboring, presumed upon

another or is, one might say, imagined,
thought turned and turned along this thread of causes,
reasoning backward, the ring of steel on steel,

the sudden hiss of the fired blade plunged in water.
"*This is the spring,*" then, carbon scale flaking
away like salt from breaking waves, her touch

reoccurring, fingers curled only slightly,
the water at her feet whitening with air, doves'
cries all around, lost to the sea's incessant clamor.

Bellows lift and fall; charcoal chimes, brightens,
and shimmers as though lit from within, its surfaces
still black, qualities, then, darkness a property

of light, his hands, arms and face red and bright
with sweat; fire, strike, fold and strike again,
spark-quick, steel turned and hammered across steel.

II.

An infinitude of measures, each grown
narrower as it is succeeded by another
and another, the arc of things parceled out;

song and dance, how the hand extended
as the body turns moves in the brightening
lilt of air, the wind sweep of gulls' wings,

the complex curve the tip of a stirring branch
heaves, hesitates and returns, chest and shoulders
lifted into music, tortoise shell scraped and strung,

its chords sprung up like waves in a freshening
wind, the billowing of sails and cumulus clouds
progressively sectioned toward area and volume.

Consider the pendulum, momentum in
moments, moment, or the sling's deliberate
sway, its smooth stone, at once fast and loose.

Only an approximate line remains,
something, more likely than real, pencil dots
to glide and turn a French curve toward,

its inside and outside scroll work, transparent
and elegantly unsatisfactory; dreams
bend their own approximations around us,

memory's turn and slope, a sentence unfurled
like dyed silk in chill water, colors at once
running away and made permanent, set.

III.

Sky blue, this fountain—light—one moment
and then another, a single droplet
its bright occasion, occasions—how many,

or how often and at what variance?—
time narrowed, drawn like wire from gold—
light, again—the taut string humming,

soft-lifted, hair or lyre, soft voice, tabla;
between the note anticipated
and the note played, what we hear is not

necessarily what occurs; song is
its own spaces drawn together, sounds
we propose amid their own inherent

silences; rest, at rest, count it out,
breathe and count, keep time, the antiphon,
light and song or light in song, "no doore

can keep them out;" days pass into night;
songs are exhausted in song, processions,
selves conceding to selves as note to note;

or Antiphon himself pressing triangles
toward the circle's edge, a near infinite
number of bases halved and moving outward

until they seem indistinguishable from
the arc itself, radians like bits of time
parceled out, one after another, in turn.

Michael Anania

IV.

Light reflected from Gold leaf is yellow,
but transmitted, by holding a leaf
of Gold twixt your eye and a candle,

is blue; *lignum nephriticum*,
sliced thin and suspended in *faire* water,
reflects blue but transmits Gold,

Hispaniola's contrary light, chill lumens
in sweet wood; Newton held this much
of the New World at eye-level,

the spirit's opposite, perhaps, or two
realms each seen through the other,
as sky to gold or gold to sky, our place

at the hour glass's neck, the iris
itself narrowing between two volumes
of light, each held in place for its moment;

this is the Spring, gold and blue, old world
and new, in which our sun, might be
confounded, its space drawn inward.

Threnody

How do we move from
sorrow to sorrow,
from grief to grief—

as finches move in flight
from struggle to glide
to struggle, clutching

at the air's brief substance
or as gulls gracing the wind
or nightbugs mad for light?

Loss is how things work;
passing, they say, into
what is, at every moment,

becoming the past.
Things spin around us,
and we spin with them,

tatters flung among tatters.
At some distance, fray
appears to be line,

scatter and swirl circle,
speech catches in the throat,
vision curves backward,

breath consumes breath.
Places matter because
they seem to endure,

city, street, plaza,
landscape, willow tree,
water faucet, headstone.

Apprehension is
constant, fear each
evening's parallax;

shades and shadows
change places; names,
like keepsakes, relics

in time, lifted and held
into the darkness that
is, as always, impending.

Three Variations on Passages from Francisco Quevedo

I.

moisten your hand, touch the ashes,
then lift their stain up to your face, rub
your thumb against your finger, grit
subsiding to an odd slick, eased there,

something akin to desire's remembered
dampness, its warmth, love, that is,
provoked from nothing, or rather,
out of chill vestiges, exhausted

fires, memory, inert, still, death's
simple chemistry; who was it tended
the drip of water through potash

into pale tallow, stirred one into
the other, wary of the sting of it
and of the coals burning red at her feet

II.

consider the inward turn her wrist
makes, the line from the outer edge
of her arm to the curve where her
fingers end and the external world

begins or the blue shadow, the fold
at her neck, say, skin's mute radiance—
ah, Orpheus, my apologies!—all turns
by turns in turnings disarrayed;

movement, the quick of her, touched,
sensed, certainly, but unknown, envied,
like the soul, then, only visible when it stirs

a feather or flares its moistures across silvered
glass, tongued like speech empty of syllables,
its swirling sentences like fire in motion

III.

by sight or reason or sighted reason,
the elevation of sun or star, charted;
can you imagine these imaginary lines,
land and ocean parceled out, parsed,

as though what we might say is
a place we occupy, or places one
after another, plottings struck along
a line, curving only slightly, grief,

how is that to be calculated, then,
with compass and sextant, tables
filled with days and times, progress

and loss; listen, listen, we are spent
in both shrieks and murmurs, ask
for both permanence and change

Michael Anania

Fragment

we are accompanied by
    sorrow, as wind to cloud
        or shadow to evening;
absence has weight; it sits
    there in the dark, one
        nothing shaping another

Cinema Universale

In those days, there were continuous showings;
you simply went to the movies, whenever you liked,
noon to midnight. An usher with a flashlight

and wearing a uniform would walk you down
the aisle, the flashlight forming an ellipse across
the figured carpet just ahead of his feet,

and people would stand up in sequence;
"excuse me," you were expected to say,
the movie, *in medias res* and Technicolor,

was directly in front of you, and in
that awkward moment, leaning slightly forward,
sliding your feet sideways so that you wouldn't

step on the toes of people whose fronts your back
was brushing against—"pardon me," "excuse me"—
trousers, jacket, sweaters, blouse fronts, ties

whispering, you seemed about to fall into it,
the movie, that is, those monumental
faces, a bosom rising, lips drawn up

into a famous pucker, kisses as
real as Monument Valley, the sudden
brightness of bright places flashing all around,

Frank Sinatra and Doris Day, for example,
his cigarette and her smile, and Gig Young,
completely out of his depth, as out of place

as you were, tilting toward them, not yet
part of the audience, a participant of sorts
in the same way someone edging across

a high window ledge participates in air.
Sitting, taking your seat, was like being
pulled back into the shadowed safety

of the ordinary room inside the window,
and the picture became, in short order,
a story, its middle proposing a beginning,

a world of commonplace occurrences in
which Doris Day moved about apparently
unaware that she was Doris Day

and Sinatra was eased into town
like a gunslinger, something only he
and Ethel Barrymore knew from the start,

and loving them both equally, regretting
Gig Young's broken heart, you knew with Ethel
that it would come out badly in the end,

that, in time, song wears away at its singer
as death unsteadies the gunslinger's hand;
how many cigarettes and how many saloons,

how many fingers of red-eye, how many
Dorothy Malones, town after town?
You wait for it, then, her sorrow and his

moment of sacrifice, each ennobling
the other, then sit through the credits,
the newsreel, the previews and the cartoons,

wait for the curtains to be drawn across
the screen, for the opening, rippled there,
first, on velvet, then, as the velvet retracts,

shimmered on a pale, riffling scrim.
And it begins again, the song swelling
as the picture clears, the dense, certain

Sinatra of the fifties, "if you are among
the very young at heart," the sleepy town,
Elmwood, Lynchfield, Tombstone or Vera Cruz,

waiting as green felt awaits the turning cards.
Is he the jack of diamonds or the knave
of hearts, the singer whose liquid song

moves now along the unsuspecting streets.
The opening is what you had imagined,
each character held briefly in the light,

friendship betrayed for love, sense for song.
This is where you came in, so you stand up—
"pardon me," "excuse me"—lifting yourself

into the moment when her mouth tilts toward his,
moving sideways across their faces, their
brief kiss briefly shadowed by your sleeve.

Outside this Orpheum, where the marquee
jitters above the sidewalk's random quartz;
you hunch your shoulders against the cold

and move into the continuous city,
streetlights evenly spaced, the first traces
of snow wisping across damp brickwork,

the same snow Sinatra, knowing he was
wrong for Doris Day, drove himself into.
Buses chatter by, like film, their windows passing,

one frame at a time. Lives move along,
each one storied in its own way, each
set of causes briefly joined here, between frayed

pasts and improbable futures, in one moment
as coherent as snowflakes joined in lamplight,
their swirl and drift ordered into bright circles.

Continuous showings continued behind you;
the continuous, causal world went on
framed windows moving their silhouettes

homeward, the squared sidewalk reeling forward,
snowflakes spun like dust motes dancing in arc light.
It was 1954, the year stop signs went

from yellow to red, and the Russians got
the Bomb, and the heart, at least according
to Sinatra, was what mattered most,

the place where love found its home or the place
it threaded its way toward like film
sprocketed, turn after turn, into the light.

II

Farm Machinery in a Vacant Lot

weld lines on drive wheels,
rust and mid-summer weeds,
the drag grader cattywompus,
its iron seat turned sideways,
a Case one-bottom pull-plow;
green enamel dulled toward grey,
Farmall red gone to burnt orange,
an Oliver horse drawn sulky-plow,
black as a dutch oven, two-row
cultivator and spring-toothed
harrow, an angled, one-knife
sub-soiler and squat New Holland
baler, all set out in the space
between empty storefronts,
unmarked, merely at rest here,
unlikely, as though collected
to some purpose and then
abandoned, toothed cutters,
sprung and ratcheted lift handles,
reaper blades, linchpins, spare parts,
shears and wheel bands scattered
among cordgrass and bottlebrush;
work is sketched out here in iron,
and forged steel, a hand at each blade,
knees and shoulders greased and bent,
the day-long clatter, jostled plow seat

31

Michael Anania

sprung on a single steel leaf, reins;
blackened with sweat and lather

    traffic eases along
    this main street, its commerce
    long gone; nobody goes
    to town anymore; they shop
    at malls two or three
    villages west, out where
    the superhighways whine
    all day and night like tree locusts;
    beyond their farm-sized parking lots
    cul de sacs multiply across
    corn stubble and buffalo grass,
    so many Fairviews, Hudson Heights,
    Clear Creeks and Deer Runs
    named, like cars, from lists of
    genial falsehoods; there are
    no views and no heights;
    the creeks have all been diverted
    and the deer run off or harvested

William Seward, Lincoln's
Secretary of State, said
that because of the reaper
"the line of civilization

moved westward thirty
miles a year"; Cyrus McCormick
took it to heart and made
an advertisement out of it:
"Westward the Course of Empire
Takes Its Way with McCormick
Reapers in the Vanguard";
and Deering's platform reaper
and John Deere's forged-steel
self-polishing plow faces,
"unshorn, boundless and beautiful,"
the prairies turned, thirty miles
each year, shoulders bent over
the sulky plow's sideways seat,
over the harrow's sprung teeth,
disks polished furrow after furrow,
the lowered cutter's steel blades,
sheaves machine-gathered and bound

Michael Anania

La Loma del Cruz

for Alice McGrath

i.

the projector chatters, waves fall;
       the movie plays out against
              smoke and mist, its storylines
barely visible; this is the end
       of the world, the usual chase on
              horseback past familiar boulders,
a stand of cottonwoods, the trail
       west hovering amid gunsmoke
              and hoofbeats, the Pacific reined in,
white froth and Stetsons; it was one
       of those evenings in Los Angeles,
              he said, when the wings of uncertain
angels struggle like tattered sails
       against unsteady, off-shore breezes,
              tides and the way things are, six-guns
and lever-action carbines, *The Phantom
       Stage Coach*, ironclad, heaves its riches
              toward Stockton, Gene Autry giddy
with nitrous oxide, Jane Russell sent
       by Howard Hughes, Billy the Kid
              trembling with a fever only her ample

breasts could hope to cure, an Indian
    blanket drawn over them as the scene
        fades to black, was it love, after all
or merely pity, *caritas*, "it was she
    who sent for me," the fallen woman
        fallen just outside the swinging doors,
a saloon piano clinking against
    the sea's murmur, the girl from the East
        in the West, speaking now, as always,
for peace and justice, a simple sense
    of what is right, her starched gingham
        unadorned, her eyes raised in hope;
are they illusions, then, ghosts
    opposing ghosts, each Saturday
        matinee recalled and cast seaward
into salt spray, our celluloid selves
    increasingly unsteady, light and shadow
        moving along moving vapors

ii.

pachucos in silhouette ("your boys,"
        you called them), angled shoulders jutted
                out, pant legs pegged tight at the ankles,
stepped out across the frame, the story
        kicked sideways, hands, radiant
                crosses in India ink, affronts on all sides;
caló, words their own mothers
        wouldn't recognize, flicked out,
                rhymed, like switchblades, sudden
and lethal sounding, posed against
        the faltering movie, against its
                devotees; being 'other' is style
and consequence, wide *pachuca* slacks,
        high-waisted and swaying, their hair
                piled up and gleaming, "catch me
if you can, *batos*," lips bright red, skin
        like polished copper, the dance is wide
                and territorial, flail and certainty,
"*¿que pasiones?*" (not "*¿que pasa?*"),
        what passions, now? moment
                to moment, a verb for ordinary
occasions, hand in hand, crosses joined
        at their bases, each set of inked radians
                passioned there, as well, *mi calabaza*

iii.

what blooms in this green field,
        wild licorice, sweet alyssum, or Tom's
                favored moss rose and begonia?
"even the flowers and the birds
        here speak English," pepper tree,
                bitter cherry, western laurel, ash;
behind you, Junipero Serra's ninth
        mission and its cross, a fashion now
                in tract houses and mansions alike;
everything is feigned, the land
        itself marked by imaginary hooves,
                one cowboy after another, one
gunshot for vice, one for virtue,
        white hats and black, ricochets
                in the box canyon, buckboard
princess leaning forward, reins
        slapped hard against a team
                of lathered horses; her breasts,
urgent, sway toward us; The Kid
        once again, in Lincoln County
                or Culver City, draws and falls;
soldiers and sailors, escorted by
        the police, pulled *pachucos* from
                dance halls and movie houses,

tore off their zoot suits, beat
    them into the streets, meting
        out the difference between
outlaw and outsider; Billy, Jane,
    Hawkes, Hughes, Pat Garrett, all
        part of the familiar script, etched
into our dreams, one Kid
    after another, forty-seven
        in all, each one quick-
handed, each loved in turn,
    in time Newman and Brando,
        Audie Murphy, an actual
hero, played himself, then
    Billy the Kid, awarded one
        star after another, Gail Storm
chaste, certainly, but smitten,
    a grateful nation and Garrett
        reluctant, as ever, to see him fall

In Any Event

"the poetics of this situation ..."

1.

sub-zero, once
again, Charles,
and the world
around us, re-
invested with
snow, its light,
a blue-tinged
whiteness, sea
blue or sky
blue scattered
unequally
and clamoring
its incidental
pieties

2.

shoulders hunched
into a cold wind
the prairie hones
eastward, its edges
drawn across rivers,
fields, treelines,
lake water freezing
a shadowed calm out
from the shoreline,
fifty feet at least, gray
lustrous and still,
the city's weights
and moments certain
and out of reach

3.

out of collision:
diffraction, corona,
brightness and color;
smoothness as easily
hued from pollen
or water droplets,
their radiance seen
merely as radiance
rather than as myriad
occasions, each one
multiple in its bright
consequences, known
and named by what is
left behind, *vestigia*

4.

reconsidered as
spheres of light,
they curve and fold
inward as skin might
curve, enclosing
its own moisture,
radiant, as well,
its heat kept almost
secret there, vein-
blue and pulsing,
speech not yet speech,
sibilant and uninflected,
chill light and distant
places held fast

Without Reason

for Giovanna Fozzer

this week the spiderwort
    is in bloom, its long stem rising
        from a loose tangle of grassy leaves,

its flowers, here at least, soft
    purple and star-petalled, still
        wet with last night's rain, lolling

in this morning's breeze, Easter
    Sunday, in fact; they will close
        as the sun brightens over them,

re-open to evening or overcast
    skies, their affinity for shade
        part of the magic implied by *wort*,

from the Anglo-Saxon, *wyrd*,
    meaning, *root*, or simply, *plant*,
        yet all the *worts* seem strange,

toxic and curative, the spider's
    root, a figure drawn, I suppose,
        from leaves arched to the ground

43

like spider's legs, or the spider's
　　word, spoken in fine threads spun
　　　　from leaf to stem, rainwater and light

caught there, nouns evaporating,
　　like speech, itself, mere breath passing,
　　　　its music as certain as its

momentary sense; lean over it,
　　and its bright filament vanishes
　　　　into your shadow, the delicate

purple flower opening toward you,
　　as heliotropes open toward the sun;
　　　　you are a cloud, then, or vespers

This and That

In January, a slight rain in the air, more mist than rain, really,
   though enough to accumulate, in time, into droplets
   that run down the windshield, the wind out of the
   northwest, steady and chilling; elsewhere and at
   another time in his life, this would have been snow,
   spinning on, rather than falling through, the air;
the announcer on the radio, which had been playing nothing
   worth mentioning or even noting, announces Julie
   London's "Hot Toddy"; or does he announce it or
   merely say, "Julie London" and play the song, the
   coolly scatted version—*one one-two-three, one one one-
   two-three, one two three*, though she says *do do-do-do,
   do do do-do-do, do do do*, except midway through the
   song when she, quite poignantly, changes to *oo oo-oo-
   oo, oo oo oo-oo-oo, ow ow ow*;
those among you concerned with narrative, as so many seem
   to be these days, will notice that the shift from *do do*'s
   to *oo*'s and *ow*'s is manifestly narrative, as all changes,
   even in music, inevitably tend to be, and referential—
   oo and *ow* as parts of pleasure and pain or pleasure
   edging toward pain or pain superseding pleasure, as
   a droplet exceeds mist, though it proceeds from it,
   offering a sense of direction to what had otherwise
   seemed a mere condition of the air;
questions of attraction, he supposed, were generated out of
   the peculiar puzzle of desire; how is it one thing, out

45

of so many, takes on such importance, as though life
without it would seem less than life, or perhaps, in
the moment, at least, less complete;
it would be simpler, he thought, to suppose that desire, itself,
is a condition, rather, that is, than an occurrence,
since it manifests itself so broadly and at such diverse
times; if it is mere absence, and absence is the
continuous companion of presence, then to perceive
presence would be to perceive absence and, therefore,
desire, as something more significant than mere appetite,
or perhaps not;
whatever is missing, as a general fact of presence and absence,
would not account for desire's specificity, a desire
not for anything or any one member of a category of
things but for one thing, one person, receptive, in a
similar state of unaccountable need;
does it matter, he wonders, that Julie London played a nurse
in a 1970s television program about paramedics,
called *Emergency*, that she took down vital signs over
a short-wave radio and said things like *saline*, *D5W*,
and *lidocaine*, that she wore white, as nurses still did
in the days before pastel, flowered scrubs, that she
seemed, even there, in costume, larger than life, that
her husband, Bobby Troup, played a doctor on the
show, which was produced by her ex-husband, Jack
Webb;

it is easy to imagine her on the set, then, microphone in
    hand, haloed with desire, Webb's pushed, we suppose,
    into the past, Troup's more recent if not as persistent,
    Webb reaching across time to dress Julie in stiffened
    white cotton and polyester, saying *pulse* and *blood
    pressure*, or *oo oo* and *ow ow* in the thick, low, desire-
    laden voice she was famous for.

Michael Anania

Second Thoughts

Desire is the fate of
place and its beginning,
the reach need gives
to fingertips and teeth,

breath's second self
warm and breathing,
the *I* in each *you*, I
say, for convenience's

sake, the locus of self
brimming with pasts,
lifting like waves and falling,
skin chilled and drawn

toward each occasion
of touch, accidental,
of course, and incertain,
the temper of things.

Celan

does enumeration itself
   propose consequence, does
      each rose fall to roses

as it is counted, the first
   Cyrillic, the second, inscribed,
      does it matter, is it matter, each

opens in its own time,
   its petals pressed outward,
      no one, nothing, time-lapse,

these vain ardors, each
   bitten in its turn, caught
      there, what was it she said

of the poets and their
   spaces, not contradiction,
      not so much sleep as waiting

Michael Anania

Acting Up

> "*I have been having great doubts about the current emphasis on Space.*"
> —Fumiki Takamatsu (1973)

i.

the point is
no space, just
mere location

the line, ex-
tension without
breadth; neither

exists, of course,
as you and I
exist, or I

exist proposing
you, a mere
location, the point,

coordinates
you pass without
incident, locus

of all those
anticipated
conjunctions,

as in or for
example, wavelet,
bouy, drift-

net or crystal
lattice, its
coarse, courses

by landfall,
soundings in
feet and fathoms

sudden as ever,
the seaway
dissipating

Michael Anania

ii.

so your foot
strikes pebbles
or crunches white

sand, the salt marsh,
itself an ordinary
occasion, sea flowers

treeline, granite
outcropping,
another horizon

tilted in its own slow
time; "take it back,"
she says, "take

it all back," as
though the speech
balloon could be

sucked back into
your mouth like
bubble gum, thought's

fair-weather cumulus
cloud vanishing with-
out consequence, so

much happens; this this
is one day, this the next,
moment to moment,

the neurons flashing
like neon, words or mere
breath, sigh and sigh

again, just for effect
(there is no audience),
Bravo! Brava! instances

of operatic virtuosity
amid such predictable,
occasions, sickness,

betrayal and death
rumors chorusing
around us once again

Michael Anania

iii.

location, *locus of
all points*, though
when you spin a thread

around your finger,
the weight at the end
speeds and spirals

inward; self, then,
the point, pointing
outward and centering,

plié, as though what-
ever moved toward
you curved inward,

however slightly, as
your attention
moves toward it, space

in all its contingencies
bending its own shape
to your slightest touch

Proximities

I.

plus or minus the quantity—
or all things being equal—
light, as you might have imagined,
quick and for our purposes
linear and entirely accessible—
the day is its usual tangle,
colors of all sorts, shades, hues;
things move apparently at random,
though everything seems purposeful,
or is it that seeming is itself
a kind of purpose, the likely
outcome of being seen, however
much seeing might, in the end, seem
to be occasioned by its own accidents

II.

a cascade of causalities
or cascading effects, river-
eddy, snow-swirl, the city's
implausible accumulations,
traffic, its busy stasis, lives,
selves trembling, purposes
adrift; "from where I stand,"
as though identity rested
on its own tripod and panned
the ingathering scene, faces,
arms and legs moving through light
and shadow, bright grillwork, fenders
curving forward, their sudden volumes
like clouds, liquid and impending

III.

all that is at rest moves, of course,
motion being the ordinary state
of things; the night turns, shadows
contract, then expand, wavelets lift
and fall into waves, each one of them
circling forward, moth-powder, smoke
trails, dust motes churning in lamplight,
the slow lift and fall of sleep, eyelids
busy at their own jittering scenes,
a persistent fidget, tangling memory
with desire; *dream along with me,*
landscape and body heat, I am no
more certain than you are, of what moves with
us through the unsteady lift of breathing

Michael Anania

IV.

for L. G.

it wakes on its own, doesn't it,
and presses its weight against you,
the incurling wave's salt edge
or a sudden breeze across sun-
tightened skin; different, certainly,
than memory's persistent longing
or the familiar grasp of need; quiet,
itself, speaks, hissing in your ear,
the sound of nothing going on
between breath and breath, restless;
belongs, you say, out there, named
and placed at some discreet distance,
an object you might, in time, turn to,
part of what seems, as you touch it, real

This Cup

for Charles Newman

I placed a coffee cup
on Jhumpa Lahiri's
sweater set (*NY Times
Book Review,* 4/6/08)
and round it was, the stain

of it, that is, and dark,
and despite her bright eyes,
her modest, round earring
and stern but endearing
refusal to smile, thought

of William Gass' *Willie
Masters' Lonesome Wife,*
the first edition where
coffee cup rings mark
the text and margins

(*Tri-Quarterly,* 1968),
at random, as though some
careless reader had put
his cup down here or there
willy-nilly, though the text

Michael Anania

begins to gather itself into
the rings and eventually
comments on them, so it's
the writer not the reader
or the writer as reader

who was careless or perhaps
deliberate and careless
or deliberately careless
with his cup; "this is
the moon of daylight"

one says; another speaks
in fragments of coffee,
in fact—"in early morning coffee
down the little sterling ide of"—
as calculated as such things

inevitably are in fiction,
even, or especially, when
their beginnings seem simple
and more or less accidental—
"the muddy ring you see

just before you and below
you represents the ring
left on a leaf of the manuscript
by my coffee cup," a reminder
(sometimes we need one) that there

was a time of composition
that preceded the book,
its duration different
in so many ways from the duration
of reading, though each, reading

and writing, can be put aside,
each ringed by its own
neglected cup, the circles
left there imposing an order
of their own, ungrammatical

and asyntactic, something
the text seems to rise up toward,
the urgent way that messages
rise through the inky black of
an eight ball to tell us the future,

advise the love-sick, heart-
weary and lonely, letters, words
pressed against the ball's small,
dark window so briefly
it is often hard to be sure

what you read there—"Outlook
good," "Signs point to yes,"
 "Most Likely," "As I see it,
yes," "It is decidedly so,"
"Reply hazy, try again."

The book's last coffee stain
encircles the navel of the nude
who has been posing (hard
to imagine these days) or as
the author might say, representing,

page after page, the title's,
if not his own, lonesome wife.
And the stained sweater set,
not the sweater set itself
or Jhumpa Lahiri, the alluring

author with the sideways glance,
but the artifact in black and white
on newsprint wicking coffee
along its random strands of fiber,
occurs as fiction might occur

amid a tangle of causes at once
intended and accidental.
The coffee's damp expands
its ring of paper, which in turn
rises like a blister of cashmere

at once fictive and tangible,
two mother-of-pearl or plastic
replica mother-of-pearl buttons
catch the ambient light, twin
crescent moons in their own daylight.

Undivided Acts

The question of time reoccurs: relative
to what? the speaker and the questioner,
all that their shared durations shared; imagine

April in Paris, 1922, Einstein at the podium;
in the audience, Bergson raises his hand,
"Would you admit to two kinds of time"—

Le Coeur á Barbe shoved into someone's
raincoat pocket, razor, hot air balloon,
a steamship passing by, Erik Satie

at the rail, barely visible, Eluard, Ernst,
The Dance of Saint Guy, all the rage
that season, Picabia's string instrument,

literature as *LIT et RATURES*—
"physical time and personal time, what is
measured and what is experienced, known?"

"No," he said, "there is only one time, over
which the time we live has no jurisdiction."
Every duration harbors others; occasions

are mere ripples in light moving outward.
Even so, light moves in time and bends inward;
however disquieting, what we know

is neither here nor there, and intuition,
the sense that there is a world that conforms
to our recurrent suppositions and that time

envelopes us like a familiar landscape,
is act of faith based as much on perception's
limitations as its furtive accuracies.

Duchamp's *Straw Hat*, by '22, an established
sedition, the Mona Lisa's moustache,
LHOOQ, she has hot pants, *chaud au cul.*

"The Fig Leaf" superimposed over "Hot Eyes,"
the sun's face or a drawing of a rotary brake,
the leaf itself squeezed from a paint tube like icing,

the figure in silhouette, one foot propped
on a black circle, sun or brake eclipsed,
the layers clear now in slant light at the Tate.

Mme. Curie attended the lecture,
Einstein's first in Paris, but if she spoke,
it wasn't recorded. Later, she and Albert

were photographed taking a walk in the grey
Paris spring. *Il fait gris*, a quality of light
or of photo-plates in a moist season.

"What do you make," she might have said,
"of the nude man in black profile, his foot
resting on what seems to be a black sun

and of his apparent precision of gesture,
and all that stands out in relief behind him?
Is one picture painted so conspicuously

over another an act of obliteration
or an effort to make us notice in art
a curt form of relativity? Do these jokes,

even when they seem merely capricious
accidental or vulgar—*she has a hot ass*—
have their beginnings in the rules we have

so meticulously challenged and broken?"
"History might well say so, though it could,
just as easily, say that you and I were freed

to think as we did by the art and music
of the '80s and '90s. When did light become
as much the subject as what it illuminated?"

"Bergson thinks that radium proves that energy
is emitted by things themselves and sparkled
across the general darkness toward life,

an unseen kind of light, magical and creative.
After all this time, my fingers ache with it."
Or did they merely walk and say nothing.

III

Three to Get Ready

for Brubeck at 85

I.

someone let it slip, as though
a small metal object had been dropped
and rang out as it bounced across the floor,
the sounds of solidity at play, the world's
clarity, I suppose, commending itself to us,

as accidental as anything compelled by
gravity might seem, a leaf yellowed and curled
against this December morning's light snow,
twigs stiff and broken in the driveway,
one more loose sentence to puzzle over

II.

waltz is invariably concave, its spaces
stitched into the still air like pine needles,
sunflower hulls and thistle husks, the finches
grayer each day, shadows, merely, graphite
moving just there across slate-colored clouds,

"*all that you might imagine*," a lilt passing
like breath amid the ordinary swirl of things,
caught, as though in song or rather in song's
conditioned anticipations, counted out as
though its syllables were yours for the taking

III.

"where was I?"—waltz, song, sentence, gray winter
morning lifted like a scrim, birds, seeds, snow
stitched loosely across loosely woven cloth,
bright leaves and broken branches, things un-
expectedly at play, the sudden ring of objects

falling, how crystal resounds within crystal,
brass against brass or steel wound around steel,
struck just, as they say, in time, time itself
flaking, then spinning away, its bright shapes
sudden and curled outward from your hands

Michael Anania

A Most Familiar and Infallible Rule: Four Austin Pieces

for Joe and Mary Doerr

1.

Prokofiev and cactus, river-
stone cracked into the parkway,
this morning's bright cumulus
rising into a cirrus brushwork;

the dead fawn at the curbside
is just a stain now, bone fragments
and bird droppings, wisps of fur
like pencil marks on concrete;

outside the coffee bar, stray talk
and grackles; inside, laptops,
screens up, their keyboards clicking
like bugs against a windowpane

2.

"actually," she says, both hands
lifted, as though the word itself
had been caught in a cat's-cradle
she holds into the air, waiting

for her companion to reach down
through it, her own bright finger-
nails extended, and pluck the strings,
something actual humming there;

or reach through with both hands,
fingers almost Balinese, to extract
an intricate complementary web,
"I see, actually, yes, of course."

3.

is it four or ten? both, perhaps;
Mozart-quick phrases giving way
to phrases, and Haydn, as well,
picked out of time and spoken,

strings, certainly, Campion,
Picinnini and Dowland—
a wooden boat, Greek or Frankish,
its strakes held fast; or *wood* merely

or *wood* plus the Persian for *string*,
the vessel, well-founded and rigged,
like *dichtung*, then, steamed and watertight,
and so set forth, landlocked, in song

4.

if we placed three oranges
along the igneous overlay,
there where the live oaks
grapple into porous stone,

bright notes above the deep
Cretaceous grey and rippling
lake water, a kestrel sun-struck
wheeling, in its own time,

overhead, the music proposed
in geologic space and momentary
time or momentary space,
clouds adrift, and geologic time.

Michael Anania

A Transcription in Passing

for Sharon Roos

"form is cut in the lute's neck,
tone is from the bowl"
E. P., *Thrones*

I.

the wave concealed her,
  its watery veil, a white foam
    draped across the dark sea's swirl,

blue-grey shadowed
  over rock pool, scrub
    oaks and elm boughs opening;

the sky is leaden
  with them, gold light
    nonetheless, and columns gleaming,

as if an Aeolian offered
  violet and sea green,
    asphodel and broom plant

II.

as though, that is, Respighi
    read it through in pieces, Caroso
        Besard, Gianocelli, Molinaro

and Vincenzo Galilei,
    the father of Galileo, in
        period notation, equal

strings with measured
    weights asway and plucked
        in octaves, four times the number,

not, as any Pythagorean might
    have supposed, two, contrary
        that is, the household humming it

III.

did Galileo *On Motion* begin
    there, among his father's weights
      and lute strings, the kitchen itself

a musical instrument drawn
    by gravity toward harmony, "toward heavenly
    harmony," not so much what falls

but what is suspended; *terminus*
    in fretwork is the ordering of song;
      planets dance, child's play, swaying;

ayrs set to numbers, numbers
    in air, the lyric of propositions,
      if, then, what, their forms melodic

IV.

disturbances, as breath
 to leaf or wind to water,
  as string to the carved bowl,

"skin to fingertip," light
 moves us, sounds, at once
  balanced and arbitrary,

an architecture in time
 transmitted by air, its forces
  drawn out in even numbers,

each dying fall, both cause
 and consequence, each string,
  angled, each angle resolved

Michael Anania

Spruce Canyon Studies

I.

in or around
   this afternoon's
      quiet, Block or Bartók

proposes a sudden
   urgency, as though
      things were more likely

or more fully lit now,
   their edges sharpened
      in the trembling air

II.

the image of self
  is coinage, merely,
    an arbitrary marker

whose value changes,
  though its denomination
    remains the same, so seems

permanent and reliable:
  can you stay awhile or leave
    some token warming in my hand

III.

it is terribly brief, isn't it,
    the duration of sound in air,
        and yet there is always sound,

the steady hum of things,
    wind, wave, traffic, the sixty-
        cycle murmur of light bulbs

and transformers, armatures
    spinning their own tunes,
        coils and magnets vibrating

IV.

these words are occasions,
 disturbances in air, cats' paws
  rippling across rippled water; still

it's the tune that proposes
 the sentence, its melody,
  implicit, though incomplete,

always; you sing along,
 word by word, within another's song
  drawn by the satisfying arc of melody

V.

it was Bartók, I think,
    "measures drawn past endurance,"
        Leinsdorf, his hands reaching out

beyond their reach toward flight;
    the bird feeder in the live oak swaying
        with the push of departing birds,

leaves as sharp as laurels, branches
    scaled with green moss, light, as well,
        and shadow and cloud-rush and sky

Just So

the mind at seventy,
or mine, at least,
darts here and there
unexpectedly;

driving west this
afternoon against
the Texas sun, I thought
of Wingy Manone,

the one-armed trumpet
player, though more
of his name than of his
one arm or his trumpet

Michael Anania

Watching the Banana Tree Grow

Las hojas del banano
vuelven verde la sombra.
—Octavio Paz

whatever stirs beyond
    your wall—sandals scuffing
        uneven cobblestones,

the diesels' idle tympani,
    broom straw drawn across
        painted concrete, the hum

of steel strings and clotheslines,
    hands sifting through ground corn,
        quick words and stray sentences,

the salt lift and sigh of
    sea water, footprints hissed
        away, cloudplay, foam—

stirs within the ribbed leaves
    of the banana tree and trembles
        through its greening shadows

Poinciana

for Don Rose

the Pershing Hotel was not
   on Pershing Road but on South
      Cottage Grove, and like so many

notable places in jazz, it no
   longer exists; in 1945, Bird was
      photographed at the door, his sax

in a blonde case, Von Freeman
   and his brothers, Dizzy, as well,
      the flame trees Ahmad Jamal

fingered into blossom there,
   in 1958, that chill January night,
      chord by tropic chord, tremble still

Michael Anania

Concerning Accident

farfalle vivaci l'attraversano
—Montale

i.

for my part, at least,
    it is song that draws
        the stray pieces in;

when or *as* struck
    like chords and what
        follows seems necessary,

inevitable even,
    words and objects, an arm
        so pale it might have been

a thin line of sea froth,
    shadowed briefly by
        wheeling birds, the press

of one word against
    the next, an incoming
        rush, clouds sun-struck

ii.

Palamedes drifted
    and radiant Julia,
        the way of things,

bright sulfurs
    at play in sunlight,
        leaves, Cecilia's song;

it's hard not to
    imagine their flight
        as having at least

the implicit intent
    of melody, a desire
        to execute one pattern

and then, as if
    causally, another
        varied in intricate

measures; breezes; *I
    am drawn to nature,*
        she said, song, its airs

move through us;
  hearing is one thing,
    listening another;

Io, Polyphemus
  and Luna, the long
    stretch of stars emerging

MORNING JAM: A SUITE

Tuesday Morning

for Garin and Shadla

I dreamed I saw
　　Ray Brown last night,
　　　　the fingers of his right

hand as light-filled
　　as pin feathers in flight,
　　　　his left hand measuring

out the limestone-
　　fissured strata of
　　　　sound, one note

after another, land-
　　scape and song
　　　　entirely coincident

Blue, Again

Wednesday morning—it's
   Miles again, this time
      in Texas, the Gulf clouds

dense grey, running
   westward, *flamenco*
      sketched in rubble stone,

not as a dancer moves,
   quick and equestrian,
      but as a hand moving

line by line across paper,
   the soft sounds of graphite
      or silverpoint catching

broken, random fibers;
   Coltrane, Evans, the dancer
      poised as though of memory

Thursday's Child

the intricate work of live
    oak trees in sunlight, one
        hard-edged shade after another,

branches shagged with pale
    green moss; random play
        within a limited field, then,

leaf, leaf cluster, light,
    shade, shadow and act,
        wave and particle,

John Lewis and Milt Jackson,
    morning places you at such
        infinitesimal distances from

consequence, precision
    seems the natural way things
        choose to be ordered, touch

the table edge as though it
    too were an instrument, cup,
        glass, bowl and spoon, a single

blackberry stem etched, like
   punctuation, into the saucer's
      pale rim; leaves, as I said, and branches

At Least

voices beyond the wall,
    Spanish, probably, the cast
        of morning shadows, Friday,

white vinca blossoming,
    cannas; Stan Getz drawing out
        one silk thread after another,

its cloth fallen into bright
    remnants, Oscar Peterson,
        and J. J. Johnson, the Opera House

in September, its arcade,
    suddenly aeolian, the dark
        river flecked with city lights,

Harry Callahan's collage
    Chicago, 1957, pieces
        not quite joined; somehow

everything you imagine,
    José Jesus Flores and his blue
        Mercury hardtop, the London House,

Eleanor on the damp slope
  of the Polk Street Bridge:
    is it *Yesterdays* already?

Saturday, In Turn

ruby-throated, this
    morning's hummingbird
        trembling at the yellow

hibiscus, a cartoon
    quarter-note just
        played; Coltrane

and Monk at the Five
    Spot, 1957, New York's
        Ruby aflame and spinning

past the subway stairs,
    Eighth Street, the city's
        dank underground breath

riffling her skirt,
    her high heels spiking
        the damp pavement, Shadow

Wilson and Wilbur Ware,
    heel tap and the taut seams
        of her figured stockings,

"My dear," someone said,
    as though in passing, as much
      breath and touch as speech

IV

Omaha Appendices: I

for Dominic Anania

Was it at the Pine Board Lounge,
with its Hammond B electric organ
or the Music Box, that Orville Bitney
threatened to kill my cousin Dominic?
I should have somehow recorded the story,
kept notes, at least, the names anyway, now,
with time, slipping out of reach. Meyer
Lansky ran a dog track in Council Bluffs
and paid my Uncle Frank to slip discount
coupons for the track into the newspapers
he sold at the corner of Sixteen and Farnum.
Lansky lived in the Paxton Hotel just two
blocks away and shot pool at the Paxton Billiards
on Douglas Street, where my father ran
numbers, shined shoes and dealt poker.
This was some time before my father's cousin,
Ralph Bonacci, slipped and crushed his legs
under the car he had just lifted off
his brother, Angelo, so some time before
Ralph opened his own news stand in front of
the drugstore at Twenty-fourth and Farnum
and after Lansky closed the dog track
and set off for fame and fortune in Las Vegas.
Angelo Bonacci had a gas station
on North Sixteenth Street; Angelo Anania,

not my father but Dominic's father,
had a gas station, also on Sixteenth Street,
but further north, almost to Locust Street
in the neighborhood where Bitney lived,
and where I saw Orville in the late fifties,
sometime after his famous courthouse jailbreak,
pulling his son past the Reed's ice cream stand,
in a Radio Flyer red wagon; it was
somehow so touching to everyone there
that day that the notorious Bitney
could be, even momentarily, fatherly
that the story was told again and again
by people who could not possibly have
been there. "Whatever you say about him,"
they'd say, "Orville Bitney was a good father.
I remember seeing him one Saturday morning
pulling his son all the way to the ice
cream stand and back in a red wagon
even though he was a wanted man
and every cop in town was out to get him."
I should have asked Dominic whether
the Pine Board or Music Box episode
happened before or after the famous
jailbreak when Bitney was on the run
and whether it was before or after
the touching red wagon incident;

it was certainly after Bitney's four-year
career as a professional middleweight
in Omaha mostly and Council Bluffs—
13, 4 and 2, with 9 knock-outs—
that ended with a second-round loss
to the wholly unknown George Blackstone,
a dive, everyone said, which began
Bitney's life as a petty criminal.
"I'm going to kill you" or "I should kill you,"
he said, pressing the muzzle of his
thirty-eight into Dominic's ribs,
an organ medley or juke box playing.
"Really? Why?" And Bitney, who apparently
had no answer worth giving, put his gun
away and went back to his drink. "Did you,"
I did ask Dominic, "have a quarrel
with Bitney?" "Not as far as I know," he said.

Michael Anania

Omaha Appendices: II

Sometime around 1949
my father's cousin, Carmen Bonacci,
was accused of carrying stolen tires
(or stolen typewriters) in the trunk
of his squad car and was suspended
from the Omaha Police Department.
Carmen said that he was carrying
the tires (or typewriters) for a friend
but would not reveal the friend's name,
which made perfect sense to everyone
in the family and everyone in
the neighborhood where Carmen was known
as the most loyal friend anyone ever had.
"He would," they said, "give you the shirt off his back;
there is nothing he wouldn't do for a friend,"
but "*u bene è perdutu*," good deeds are lost.
No one thought for a minute that he
had stolen the tires (or typewriters),
and since he was never charged with theft,
he petitioned to be reinstated on the force.
On the day of his court hearing he met
the Chief of Police, whose name was Franks,
on the courthouse steps. Franks said something
to Carmen, and Carmen punched him in the mouth.
I should say here that Carmen was big, more
broad than tall, with huge arms and thick hands,

the best man, my father would say, to have
with you in a fight, one punch and the Chief
went down, bleeding. Carmen, reasoning
that the court case would, at that point, be
prejudiced against him, turned and left.
The Chief swore out a warrant for assault,
and Carmen became a dangerous fugitive.
There were stories in the newspaper;
a radio station said he had been
spotted in a bar in Kansas City,
but I saw him that very day in front
of his father's little candy store on South
Twenty-seventh Street, eating ice cream
with four or five uniformed policemen.
He gave me a Dreamsicle and a cream
soda, called me Mickey and mussed my hair.
In his own defense he said that the Chief
had sworn at him and used an ethnic slur—
"stupid fucking wop" was our guess,
though Carmen refused to repeat the remark,
not out of delicacy, I think, but because
in order present the full effect
he would have to have imitated Franks'
imitation of his stutter; "Ca-Ca-Ca Carmen"
was what he was called in school and was
still sometimes called inside the family

to distinguish him from the two other
Carmen Bonaccis in his generation,
Little Carmen and Carmen, called Muzzie.
In time, despite Carmen's reluctance,
the story of the Chief's remark got out,
and even people in the city who had
no use for "stupid fucking wops" thought
that Franks got exactly what he deserved.
"What can you expect," they said, "if you call
a dago like that a wop to his face?"
The charges were dropped, some said because
the Chief didn't want to have to repeat
what he said in court, others said that Carmen's
family had intervened with the judge.
In the neighborhood, Franks was called a "dumb
kraut" or "*pezzu di carni cu l'occhi*,"
a piece of meat with eyes, as for the police
department, "*u pisci fet d'a testa*,"
a fish starts smelling from the head; Carmen
dropped his petition for reinstatement,
bought a Texaco station on Center Street
and drove a blue Lincoln Continental
that moved through the narrow neighborhood streets
like a yacht maneuvering in a close harbor.

Omaha Appendices: III

On February 19, 1909,
a Greek, named John Mousaourides,
was stopped at Twenty-fourth and N Street
and arrested by a South Omaha
policeman, named Edward Lowery, for
socializing with a "white" woman,
by all accounts a young prostitute.
The Greek fought back, resisting arrest
and in the struggle either stabbed or shot
Lowery to death and escaped. He was
caught some time later by another
officer, named Harder, and locked up
in the South Omaha jail. One source says
that Lowery arrested the man for
vagrancy, that the man produced
a hidden revolver and shot Lowery.
In this account, but no other, Lowery
drew his own gun and as he collapsed, fired,
striking the suspect twice. Lowery was
carried, dying, to a nearby drug store.
Some Greeks said that Lowery was drunk
and that he wanted the girl for himself.
The next day a local newspaper sponsored
a public meeting to protest Lowery's
death in particular and Greeks in general.
The mayor and city council of South

Omaha attended. "One drop," one speaker
said, "of American blood is worth all
the Greek blood in the world." The crowd set off
for the jail to "get that Greek and lynch him."
The South Omaha police decided
their jail wouldn't keep the mob out
and Mousaourides in, so put him
in a wagon, wounded or not, to take
him to the much stronger jail in Omaha.
The mob followed, pulling at Mousaourides'
arms and legs and trying unsuccessfully
to overturn the wagon. Depending on
the account you read, there were one thousand,
three thousand or five thousand people
in the crowd when it turned back south
and headed for Greektown, a stretch of homes
and businesses between L and Q Streets
on either side of South Twenty-fourth Street.
The crowd attacked Greeks, beating men, women
and children wherever they could find them,
set fire to homes and looted and burned shops.
They beat, as well, several Italians
and Rumanians who were in their way
and may or may not have been mistaken for Greeks.
In a day and a night every building
in the area was destroyed and hundreds

of Greeks were out in the February
Nebraska cold, homeless. During the riot,
neither the Omaha Police nor
the South Omaha Police responded
to the Greeks' appeals for help. The next day
the Greeks were told that unless they wanted
more violence they should get out of town,
and they did, all of them, in a single
day, moving to Sioux City and Council Bluffs
in Iowa and as far away as Salt Lake City, Utah.
The Omaha Daily News said, "Greeks are
a menace to the American working man,
just as the Japs, Italians and other
similar laborers are. Their quarters
are unsanitary, and they are insulting
to women." When the news of the riot
and expulsion reached Greece, the Greek
government presented a formal complaint
to the State Department in Washington.
A lawsuit was filed that took nine years.
My grandfather, who was fifteen in
1909 and had been in America
and Omaha for just four years, took
the same lessons every other ethnic,
Italian or not, took from the Greektown
riot—work hard and keep close to your own,

expect no help from the police or the courts
and keep away from "white" people. The Italians—
Calabresi and Siciliani—pulled
their neighborhoods in around them just as
they had walled themselves into mountain
villages in Calabria and Sicily
for centuries. They lived within their own
dialects in houses that had surnames
on streets where there were no strangers.

Omaha Appendices IV

In the *Omaha City Directory*
for 1914 my great-grandfather
is listed at 2618 Rees Street
as "Angelo Anannea, laborer,"
his last name, only that one time, misspelled;
on the same page his sons are listed
at their own addresses as Dominic
and Michael Anania. It is hard
to know whether the old man, by then
already sixty-three, gave them the wrong
spelling in order to preserve the sound
of his name, which in Italian rhymes
with Pangea or Judea and not as
I pronounce it in English rhyming with
Jeremiah or if, which is more likely,
the census-taker wrote it out in what
he thought was phonetic English,
Anannea for Anania then, which may
in turn be the reason the family
in Omaha, only, adopted
the long i-sound to pronounce its name,
trading one loss for another, which is
a step you take away from yourself,
part of becoming, in time, American.
So Gigliotti became Gigliotti,
pronounced Gillottee, or Gillot pronounced

Gillat, or Gelloti pronounced Gellati,
and Pane, the two-syllable word for bread,
became the one syllable Pane, as in Payne,
and Peri became Perry; Michele,
Michael, then Mike; Domenico, Dominic,
eventually Donny; Giovanna,
Jenny; Giuseppe, Joseph, then Joe;
Giuseppina, Josie; Raffaele,
Ralph; Pietro, Pete; Francesco, Frank.
No one complained, really; what loss
there was came so easily. Italian first
names were reserved for evening whispers,
for consolations and novenas.
Sometime in the thirties a distant cousin,
named Antonio Georgioni, went
to court and changed his name officially
to Anthony George; Tony George was what
he had in mind, a real American name,
but in the neighborhood from then on
he was called "Tony the Dago,"
a comic reproach so uniformly
applied that until I was fifteen or so
it was the only name I knew for him.
Once, confounded, but trying to be polite,
I called his wife Mrs. Tony the Dago.
She scowled at me and told my father

that he had better teach me some manners.
Sometime in the forties, though Italy
remained Italy, the adjective became
eye-talian, not Italian or Italiano,
so you went to the store for eye-talian
bread or eye-talian canned tomatoes
and spoke, whenever you spoke it, eye-talian,
an insult having become the word
in American for everything you cherished.

Notes

"Casa de la Torre"

los jorobados— humpback whales

Hichol and Cora—two surviving native cultures and languages in western Mexico. The Hichol ("the healers") religion, language and art have survived into the present.

mariachis—the word is Hichol in origin.

beeswax—Hichol art uses bright yarns and beeswax to represent animals from peyote-supported rituals.

Guzman and Mendoza—conquistadors sent to subdue the native tribes of the Sierra Madres.

"Cielito Lindo"—the familiar song describes a girl who has come down from the Sierra Madres.

"white-tailed deer"—In 1988 the Hichol made a 600-mile pilgrimage to the Mexico City Zoo to acquire a small herd of white-tailed deer; they resettled the deer into their mountains, restoring, in their view, an essential order to the world.

"The Mirror of Simple Spirits"

Narcissus—Caravaggio's painting of Narcissus is in the Barberini in Rome.

"Transactions of the Ingenious World"

Title, from the cover page of Volume I of the scientific journal Philosophical Transactions (London, 1665).

Epigraph ("of stuffe ...")—John Donne.

"This is the spring in which our Sun must dy"—from Issac Newton's Alchemical Notebook, c. 1670 (Beinecke Library, Mellon

MS. 79). The spring's source is Venus.

"French curve"—the drafting tool used to draw approximations of irregular curves.

"tabla"—from David Courtney's "The Psychoacoustics of Musical Pitch."

"no doore can keep them out"—from George Herbert's "Antiphon."

"Antiphon himself"—the 5th-century-BC Sophist and mathematician who set the numerical value of π.

"Gold leaf ... *nephriticum*"—from Issac Newton's *Of Colours*. *Lignum nephriticum* is phosphorescent wood found in Mexico and first sent to Spain in 1565.

"La Loma del Cruz"

There have been 47 American movies made based on the life of Billy the Kid. Six were released in 1941, six in 1942, the year of the Sleepy Lagoon case, and seven, including Howard Hughes' movie, *The Outlaw*, with Jane Russell, in 1943, the year of the Zoot Suit Riots. Alice Greenfield (later Alice McGrath) was the model for the young Anglo woman who worked as the Executive Secretary for the Sleepy Lagoon Defense Fund and supported the *pachucos* after the 1943 riot, in Luis Valdez' movie, *Zoot Suit*. Alice's home was in La Loma del Cruz.

"In Any Event"

"the poetics of this situation"—from Charles Olson, *The Maximus Poems*, "the poetics of this situation are yet to be found out."

"Undivided Acts"

Henri Bergson and Mme. Curie were both in the audience for Einstein's first Paris lecture in April 1922.

Le Coeur à Barbe (The Bearded Heart)—Tristan Tzara's Dadaist magazine was first published in Paris in April 1922.

The Dance of St. Guy—a Francis Picabia construction of a Dadaist musical instrument, an empty frame with strings and small cardboard square with outrageous slogans, including the title.

LIT et RATURES (bed and erasure)—Picabia illustrated this Marcel Duchamp pun for the cover of *Litterature* #7 (1922).

LHOOQ—Duchamps inscription on his moustache Mona Lisa. In French LHOOQ reads as, "*Elle a chaud au cul*" (She has a hot ass, or hot pants.)

"Concerning Accident"

"*farfalle vivaci l'attraversano*" ("butterflies' bright crossings") from Eugenio Montale's "*Voce giunta con la folaghe.*"

"A Most Familiar and Infallible Rule"

Title—from a Thomas Campion book on composing for the lute.

Prokofiev—Initially *The Classical Symphony*, then *The Love for Three Oranges*.

Picinnini and Dowland—16th-century lute players and composers.

"Greek or Frankish …"— from the varied etymologies for "lute."

"*dichtung*"—-poetry, a well-fitted or well-caulked boat.

"Watching the Banana Tree Grow"

"*las hojas del banano …*" ("the leaves of the banana tree turn shadows green") from Octavio Paz's *Abol Adentro*.

ACKNOWLEDGEMENTS

Grateful acknowledgement is made to the following publications in which some of these poems first appeared: *American Letters and Commentary, Bayou, Briar Cliff Review, Café Review, The Dave Brubeck Quartet Newsletter, Denver Quarterly, Guest Room, North Branch, Notre Dame Review, The Literary Review, Iowa Review, Italian Passages, Jet Fuel, Seven Corners, Toad Suck, Tri-Quarterly,* and *VIA.*

"The Mirror of Simple Spirits" and "Concerning Accident" appeared in *Italian Passages: Making and Thinking History.*

"Farm Implements in a Vacant Lot" was first published in a portfolio by the Haybarn Press in 2009.

"Thursday Morning" was published in *Gathering: Fifteen Poets/Poems* with lithographs by Ed Colker by Haybarn Press in 2010.

ABOUT THE AUTHOR

MICHAEL ANANIA is a poet, essayist, and fiction writer. His published work includes twelve collections of poetry, among them *Selected Poems* (1994), *In Natural Light* (1999) and *Heat Lines* (2006). His work is widely anthologized and has been translated into Italian, German, French, Spanish and Czech. He has also published a novel, *The Red Menace*, and a collection of essays, *In Plain Sight*. He has received a number of awards and fellowships, including the Charles Angoff Award and the Aniello Lauri Award for poems in this collection.

Anania was poetry editor of *Audit, a quarterly*, founder and co-editor of *Audit/Poetry*, poetry and literary editor of The Swallow Press, poetry editor of *Partisan Review* and a contributing editor to *Tri-Quarterly* and has served as an advisory editor to a number of other magazines and presses.

He is Professor Emeritus of English at the University of Illinois at Chicago and a member of the faculty in writing at Northwestern University. He also taught at SUNY at Buffalo and the University of Chicago. He lives in Austin, Texas, and on Lake Michigan.

CPSIA information can be obtained
at www.ICGtesting.com
Printed in the USA
LVHW100038070422
715514LV00008B/1406

9 781941 196441